HOW CAN SINGLENESS POSSIBLY BE A BLESSING?

BY TARA EVANS

2CORINTHIANS 12:9

BUT HE SAID TO ME, "MY GRACE IS SUFFICIENT FOR YOU, FOR MY POWER IS MADE PERFECT IN WEAKNESS". THEREFORE I WILL BOAST ALL THE MORE GLADLY OF MY WEAKNESSES, SO THAT THE POWER OF CHRIST MAY REST UPON ME.

Book cover~

I chose this picture on the cover of this book to illustrate the path that God has placed me on. I know it does not look like much, but this picture signifies so much to me.

"God told me that this was my path. As God pointed to the ground He explained to me that my path will be like the pebbles and rocks on the ground. There will be pebbles that I can kick to the side, rocks that I can move, rocks that I will need to walk around and boulders that I will need to climb over." *(In God's Presence, page 92, My Testimony)*

This picture illustrates my boulder; which is singleness, loneliness, alone and this book is how God helped me to climb over.

IN DEDICATION TO:

MY LOVING FAMILY AND FRIENDS

TO MY DAUGHTER FORREST: I WILL ALWAYS LOVE YOU!

TO NEW GENESIS: I WILL ALWAYS LOVE YOU ALL, MY PASTOR, PASTORA, ELDERS, LEADERS, SERVANTS, BROTHERS & SISTERS.

TO MY SISTER FLORENCE: I HAVE ALWAYS LOVED YOU WITH ALL MY HEART! I HAVE MISSED YOU AND I LOOK FORWARD TO GETTING TO

KNOW YOU. YOU CALLED ME WHEN I NEEDED YOU THE MOST. THANK YOU SO MUCH!

TO MY SISTER RAMONA: I ADMIRE YOU SO MUCH! I COULD FILL BOOK AFTER BOOK OF THE WONDERFUL MEMORIES I HAVE WITH YOU. I COULDN'T HAVE MADE IT THROUGH MY CHILDHOOD WITHOUT YOU. YOU HAVE NO IDEA JUST HOW IMPORTANT YOU ARE TO ME.

TO MY SISTER DAWN: THANK YOU FOR BEING SO EXCITED ABOUT MY FIRST BOOK. YOUR EXCITEMENT PUT A HUGE SMILE ON MY FACE, I COULD TELL YOU ARE PROUD OF

YOUR BABY SISTER. I LOVE YOU DAWNIE!

TO MUYLY TIROLETTO: IT'S SO IMPORTANT FOR ME TO EXPRESS MY GRADITUDE TO YOU. 2014 WAS A HORRIBLE YEAR HOWEVER, YOU WERE ALWAYS THERE FOR ME WITH A KIND WORD AND A WHOLE LOT OF UNDERSTANDING. YOU ARE AN AMAZING PERSON AND I THANK YOU FOR ALL YOU HAVE DONE IN MY LIFE.

I WOULD LIKE TO SAY THANK YOU TO:

TO SHAWNA EDMONDS: THANK YOU SHAWNA NOT FOR BEING MY STYLIST ALTHOUGH

I DO APPRECIATE THAT BUT FOR BEING MY FRIEND. I SEE YOU FOR THE PURPOSE OF GETTING MY HAIR DONE BUT YOU DO SO MUCH MORE. TIMES I TELL YOU I AM TIRED WHICH I AM BUT I'M TIRED BECAUSE I'M DOWN. YOU ALWAYS PICK UP MY SPIRIT. YOU ARE AN AMAZING PERSON AND I AM GRATEFUL TO GOD FOR YOU.

TO ELLEN ABBOTT*: YOUR SUPPORT MOVED ME TO PUBLISH THE FIRST BOOK. YOU HAVE NO IDEA WHAT YOUR KIND WORDS HAVE DONE FOR ME.*

TO LYDIA DE SANTIAGO: *YOU WERE THE FIRST TO EXTEND YOUR HAND TO ME IN FRIENDSHIP BEFORE I CAME TO MY NEW OFFICE AND YOU CONTINUE TO BE THE FIRST. I WILL ALWAYS REMEMBER THAT YOU WERE THE FIRST TO PURCHASE MY FIRST BOOK.*

TO WANDA ROQUE: *YOUR SILENT SUPPORT, IS LOUD AND CLEAR. I APPRECIATE YOU VERY MUCH!*

To Wanda ~
You mean the world to me! I see you as an amazing friend. Thank you, because without you there would be many times I would not have made it. I thank God for you ~ Tara

My first book was mostly about relationships. My mind was so warped about the way I saw them and that really needed to be straighten and ironed out. I needed to know what was the responsibility for a woman and for a man in a relationship. What's going on, what's happening, what is reasonable and what is not reasonable.

I needed to really straighten out my thoughts about how to handle, deal with and change all the things that plagued my mind. Now, God has revealed all of those things to me regarding relationships. Now I have come to see that my condition at this point is being single. Not that I want to stay single or that I want to be single forever. But at this point my condition or status is single. Okay what do I do now? How is singleness a blessing for me and how do I accept this gift? How do I truly see it as a blessing, not just say it but, really feel this blessing in my heart.

I've read a few books on loneliness, being lonely and how to overcome the loneliness. All these books on the subject were wonderful books, chocked full of information. However, what I was looking for was that next step. Examples of how people get through it. What folks did in certain situations. Examples, testimonies and maybe some life stories that really dig a tad bit deeper. I was hoping for someone to get personal, get transparent, tell me, talk to me and that is what I really wanted to do this time. Really talk about being single and what does that mean. Also, talk about the fears of the thought of being married. By being single for long period of time, I became used to it, even though that's not the condition I want to be in. That is not the marital status I desire.

I want to talk about my fears and what I have experienced, what I have seen from childhood to the present. What have I seen that is kind of making me feel like "Yes, I want a husband still but maybe not right now." Also, is God telling me now is my time or now is my turn but my fears are pushing me or pulling me back? Am I being presented with good people, all good men but my fear is throwing a wall up to stop this from happening?

I wanted to really examine this issue, as well as taking a careful look at what are we doing to make ourselves feel lonely or be alone. What are we doing to ourselves that's making that happen?

Being single is a matter of marital status. I'm not a couple I'm one in that sense, I understand it makes sense to me. But just because your single it doesn't necessarily mean that you have to be alone. It doesn't mean that you have to be lonely. If you do desire a spouse in the future, you don't have to be afraid. Examine it... Look at it... Think about it... I just wanted to write about this to ease my mind, to be able again to ask God to reveal these things to me. How and what do I do to move forward to the next step, to the next leg of this race that God has prepared for me to run.

Introduction~

I believe Jehovah is having me deal with my personal issues by writing this book. It's painful and always hard to see myself in a way that I normally don't see myself. You see, God showed me who I was, oppose to who I thought I was. I think about it this way, if you look at a bell curve looking left to right, left being less toward the middle to the right being more I always thought I was on the right. Because I felt I was such a good person and I had so much to give I saw myself a different way from reality.

Now reality is I was on the left, although there were a lot of good qualities to me I wasn't the best when it came to really showing those qualities. I wasn't the best when it came to the inner person and overtime I realized that's the person that shines from the inside, that's the person that people connect with.

    I could look beautiful, show intelligence and have the best of everything but those things don't necessarily show the best of me. However, if they do, it's only the outer or the shallow parts of me. Not the inner, deeper parts of me God revealed. Who I was, His word the bible and applying the scriptures, He provided for us to live our lives. This is what moves me slightly over the top of the bell curve towards the right. However, I didn't put me there, God put me there. It's His word the bible and applying the scriptures are what puts me there. God revealed to me everything I needed to know, it's all there in the bible, all in front of us. What if we are not willing to move forward with what God has given us? That's when we get hung up.

Let me put it this way, God put in my face all these things I really didn't want to realize or see.

As I wrote my first book, I would remember stories in general. Some funny, some not so funny. "Wow! Pow! Slap!" was not so funny. However, "Circle Time" and "Relationships" were a little more humorous. Believe it or not off the top on my head I can't remember all the chapters. God made it clear to me all the questions I asked Him so the answers could be reveal to me.

What type of person I was because again saw myself just like that bell curve, I saw myself on the right side but reality was I was on the left side. It was God that brought me from the left to the right. Now, I still need to work on applying scriptures and being an imitator of Jesus Christ to be able to continuously move forward in God's service.

I think of it this way for me, I was just living my life and I was living just fine. I wasn't out there murdering anyone, hurting anyone, beating up anyone. Robbing, stealing or messing with anyone's man, at least not to my knowledge. Not hanging in the streets or in the bars getting picked up. I was sophisticated looking and I held myself as a lady. So I saw myself as doing just fine, at least this is the way I saw myself. I figured my life was just fine, at least that is what I believed.

Sometimes I try to understand things in my life by thinking out of the box a little.

Watching TV one day, I'm changing the channels and I come across an old western show.

My mind starts to think about how this show could possibly bring to my mind a lesson. Then I imagine I'm riding over bumpy terrains in a covered wagon, traveling from east to west in the 1800's. I'm all covered I'm good and what I mean is I'm good in my life. I'm protected against the weather, the rain and the wind shaking my current life, I'm good! Have a good job, home, family and things are good. Now, I'm riding and I have three wheels, three big wagon wheels, why do I care the wagon is still moving just fine. Granted not great, but fine enough it's teetering back and forth but fine just the same. It hasn't tipped over or stopped so I'm okay! Here's the thing, I'm not okay.

When I really thought about it, you know what I'm saying? There's more for me to do the more I thought about it, that wagon can move with three wheels. But how much better will it move with one more wheel? Then I thought, I've been doing fine with three wheels. The fact is, I wasn't doing fine with three wheels on my own. God has been doing for me with three wheels. But I had in my mind it was all me. Reality is it's not all me it's God. God is taking care of me and making sure I get over that terrain with those three wheels.

The time is now to allow God to step all the way in my life and be that fourth wheel. Now is the time to apply the Scriptures. Being a Christian is a lifestyle it's not just a religion, it's a relationship with God. Now He's already taking care of the three wheels it's time for that fourth wheel, to make that relationship with God and that's what I needed to do. What I'm trying to do with this book is to bring to light where I was wrong and there's a lot of us living the same life that I lead.

I wasn't happy about being a Christian at first so to speak. Because I thought I was going to lose everything about me. But then I went to a Christian woman's conference. I saw different women, different personalities, different looks and different ages. However, they all had two things in common they loved God, some women you could tell were a little bit more rocker type, some were little more conservative, some were sassy, some were maybe a little plainer and some were diva-luscious (confident, well put together) just fabulous, all so amazing. The second thing they had in common was the Lord did not require any of them to change their inner personality. God doesn't require you change your whole self and fit into a mold to serve Him. They all retained the good parts of the personality that they've always had the creativity, what makes them an individual. None of them had to change that to serve the Lord. However, what changes that did happen in their lives caused them become better in service to the Lord. Better mothers, better wives, better sisters, better aunts, better grandmothers, better cousins, better friends and better Christians. That was the best part of all.

That's what made me realize "Tara, you can be Tara you don't have to be someone else to serve the Lord". I think that's the biggest fear some women have the feeling that every part of them will be taken. That was the biggest fear I had. Since God has revealed to me what I now know and continues to reveal to me what I need to know, I feel overly blessed. I feel this is where need to be everything I wanted to do in life, God has enhanced it. He has enhanced my dreams, my goals and made one dream happen.

Yes, we have a good life but it can be better, believe it or not. You have a great life but are you living a real Christian life? Do you have a relationship with God? He's waiting on you and hopefully you answer the door when He knocks. I know I ducked and dodged that door for a long time before I answered it. Serving God starts out as a process as you learn more in your relationship with God. Then grows as you begin to progress in your knowledge of the bible. The application of the scriptures and your relationship with God as God is transforming you.

Your needs sometimes change, mines did. Now, serious contemplation of a husband, a spouse is a strong desire for me. My trust and faith is in God to find that person for me, to provide that person or prepare that person for me. But sometimes it's hard to wait. That is when we have to rely and trust what the bible has to say regarding this:

**<u>Psalm 37:4-Delight yourself in the Lord,
and he will give you the desires of your heart.</u>**

Psalm 37:5-Commit your way to the Lord;
trust in him, and he will act.

Psalm 37:7-Be still before the Lord and wait patiently for him;
fret not yourself over the one who prospers in his way,
over the man who carries out evil devices!

TABLE OF CONTENTS:

1. SINGLENESS –28 MY TEMPORARY BLESSING? 29

- But seriously, is it possible to cause my own singleness? Does this even make any sense? **34**
- So now that my eyes are open to how I looked to others, what's next? **39**
- Being patient and waiting on God is not an easy thing to do. I found that my faith was constantly tested by the enemy. **41**
- I felt at this point drawing closer to God was what I knew to do. But feeling

down not only took me away from family and friends but also God. Rekindling that love with the Lord is what was needed, then He would reveal what was next for me. **45**
- Ok, now I have a healthy view of myself but I'm still feeling a little alone. So now I'm thinking, does my behavior isolate me? **48**
- Now that I have an understanding of me, just a little, it's time for me to have more appreciation for my singleness. **61**
- Although I do appreciate singleness it doesn't stop the loneliness at times. **71**

2. LONELINESS –72 THE ACHING FEELING IN MY SOUL. 73

- The feeling of being without someone is hard enough, but what if mental health is involved? Is it harder? Or will there be compassion? **77**
- Then I think to myself, Do I cause my loneliness? 84
- What if I can't be happy for others, does that isolate me? **87**

3. ALONE – WHY DO I FEEL ALONE WHEN I HAVE GOD? 90-91

- But again responsibility time! I did as I saw, not taking the time to find the right man to have a family with if I had waited, would this be different? **96**
- There have been times where the same ole getting nowhere has put my heart and soul in a very deep dark place. And I found staying

close to good relatives and friends heled me not to check out of life. But what about those that for whatever reason don't have those people in their lives? Makes you think just how important a kind word or jester really is. *99*

- Life, sometimes seem so tough and it is so easy to hide from the world. But instead, being a part of something bigger than yourself maybe the boost that is needed to make you feel better. I defiantly did for me. *106*

4. ALONE AND MARRIED – WHAT I HAVE HEARD AND WHAT IS MY FEAR. *112-113*

- I was thinking why couples don't make it to marriage especially after being in a relationship for a long period of time? *118*
- Do I really know my roles? *123*
- Putting God first is a must! *127*
- It's been a long time coming but now I get it. *137*

CONCLUSION *143*

SCRIPTURES USED: *150*
BIBLES USED: *152*
DICTIONARIES USED: *152*

SINGLENESS

1 Corinthians 7:8-9

8-To the unmarried and the widows I say that it is good for them to remain single as I am. 9- But if they cannot exercise self- control, they should marry. For it is better to marry than to burn with passion

1. My temporary blessing?

The Merriam-website dictionary defines singleness as, the quality or state of being single. The free dictionary defines singleness this way: 1. Not accompanied by another or others; solitary. 2. Consisting of one part, aspect, or section: a single thickness; a single serving. 3. Having the same application for all; uniform: a single moral code for all. 4. Consisting of one in number; She had but a single thought, which was to escape. 5. Separate from others: individual *and distinct: Every single child will receive a gift. 6. Designed to accommodate one person or thing: a single bed.*

To start off, I would like to explain just how deep my feelings were regarding my status of being single. Before I came to God, I was not happy about being single. I felt as if you were single at my age, there was something seriously wrong with you. I had an emptiness in my heart, feeling I was not worth being loved. I remember my heart breaking because I was single. So bad I could feel a physical pain associated with this physiological pain I was feeling. With failure and disappointment, one after another I felt I had no value.

When I allowed God into my life, He put me on a necessary process of healing. God has helped me to see being single in a different way, a blessing. Things that would completely break me down and cause me to go into deep depression for months at a time no longer bothered me to that level any longer. Seeing a couple hold hands or, sharing a tender kiss would be like a knife to my heart. Why? Because this seems too silly right? Not for me, these feelings were too real and I felt like I was in an emotional fight with my lack of self worth on a daily basis.

Now I feel blessed and up lifted, being able to take advantage of looking at couples and seeing what I want and don't want when I begin my relationship. Instead of looking at a couple and being inflamed with jealousy, anger, and hatred for what they may or may not have. With God I have better opportunities to receive the person best suited for me.

Now, as for relationships, regarding how the world sees singleness. As well as how I use to see singleness. Before becoming a Christian, my only thought was going on a date and just seeing how it would turn out. The thought wasn't if this person was the one for me. It was more if we'd hit it off, then we will see where it goes. Basically, I just went with the flow not having any sort of plan. I remember caring for someone and being so afraid of really showing the person I am. The fear was, he may not want me due to this or use it to break up. I felt as if I were on eggshells. But this is something that was common with me in the past. Because I had no goal or purpose in the dating process, what should have been a wonderful experience became miserable, heartbreaking and painful.

Looking for love on dating sites was challenging I met a gentleman and he stated that he was looking for a wife and not just a girlfriend. I'm thinking to myself "This is great!" Not long after, he broke up with me stating I was not the one for him. It hurt, trust me it truly did, but I had to respect his feelings on the matter and let go. Running into him about a year later, I found he had a few girlfriends since our break up and they did not seem to fit the bill either. I came to the conclusion that it possibly wasn't me or the other ladies. Perhaps he wasn't sure of what he truly wanted and wasn't being honest with himself. In other words, he had no real purpose in the way and whom he was looking to date. Having a habit of not making a decision, this I understood because I was doing the same thing partly causing my singleness.

<u>But seriously, is it possible to cause my own singleness? Does this even make any sense?</u>

    I think about what was my last straw, so to speak when I said enough is enough and I need to make my decision to serve the Lord. I'm thinking right now this is what I love about God. He takes these situations, these events and things that happen in your life. He'll keep playing those things in your head until you get the lesson that He is trying to give you. In most cases for me this is more than one lesson per issue. At least that's what I've found.

    My rock bottom, so to speak, was with a friend of a friend. I went to his home and we ended up being together, intimately. When the morning came, I could not wait to get out of his house. He drove me home. When we got to my house, I let him know that we were never going to be together again. It was never going to happen. He was so depressed and depressing.

    Poor guy, he couldn't make a decision. He was wishy-washy, he had no confidence, no self-esteem, no nothing. But he was a good-looking guy he had a nice house and a good job, you know? Sadly, he had no problem telling you he had no money or he couldn't pay his mortgage. No problem telling you things that he couldn't do. Which really isn't an issue, but he had no plans of doing anything about it either. This man had no problems talking about it, but he couldn't make a decision as to what to do about it.

Okay, you don't have money, you have to pay this, you have to pay that, you have child support and all these bills that you have to pay. Okay, I get you! Now, what are you going to do? What decisions are you going to make so your life will be easier? Or are you just going to cry about it? I felt overwhelmed with him. I felt like, I didn't want to get stuck every time I would turn around to take money out of my pocket to pay something for him to help him out. I didn't want to do that! I wasn't willing to give up my house to move with him in his house, to help with his bills. And I didn't want him to give up his house to move with me, because I didn't know him like that. So I'm sitting here saying to myself, "Why won't this man make a decision?" This is crazy, I have no interest in this man because he will not make a decision. Not because he wasn't good looking, or a nice man, not because he didn't have a good job or that he didn't have a car and his house was gorgeous. It wasn't any of those things, it was because he was too wishy-washy and couldn't make a decision!

But here's the lesson to be learned, this is what I was showing others in a potential relationship. I couldn't keep someone in my life because, I was showing them what he was showing me. Maybe not to that level of extreme, because he was extreme. But now I saw how I was showing an indecisiveness about myself to people that I was dating. The outside was good but the indecisiveness and the inability to make a decision of any sort. Not willing to make a decision and not willing to do anything about not making a decision. Not willing to try, just kind of going through life and going through the motions. Not willing to better myself and I think that was what was so unattractive about me. But what kills me, unlike those gentlemen that did me wrong, I made it very clear to him that we would not be together again. I didn't mind us being friends but if he couldn't except that, then it was best for us to stay separate. If friendship is not good enough then I wish you well. You see, I was honest but I did not get that honesty in return. That "cut and dry" honesty, so I knew where I stood.

  God was showing me what I was showing others through this man. Honestly, being indecisive and not willing to do better. Not having any confidence, self-esteem, or self-worth. Playing the victim, and wanting everyone to feed into it, that's what makes you unattractive to someone. Crying and boo-hooing all the time, it's unattractive, it's not something you want in a relationship. I get it now, thank you Jehovah.

<u>So now that my eyes are open to how I looked to others, what's next?</u>

Sometimes we have to take responsibility for our singleness. Some of us are single for different reasons. But, I believe when you cause a level of isolation within yourself, you're causing a level of loneliness, alone or singleness to yourself. Now then, how do you get upset when no one wants to partake in your life? When you continue to be arms distance away from everybody. I've known in the past that I would be invited to all different types of events. "Tara, you want to go here?" "Tara, you want to go there." My answer was always "no". Or at the moment say "yes", but then at the last minute I would back out. Well you know what, after a while people won't ask you.

I was more depressed and more alone because people wouldn't ask me, than I was when being asked and not going. Strange, huh? I would know that the event is going on that day and I knew everybody was having a good time. I knew I was invited but I didn't go. Or, I knew all this is going on and because I said no so many times, everyone gave up on asking me.

So, in that case I isolated myself, I chose to be single but then I was upset when no one wanted to be a part of my life. You can't have it both ways, you know. I'll be the first person raise my hand and say "Yep I'm guilty of that, definitely guilty of that". I think that's what I really want to come across is that being single it is a gift. Being single what I mean is not being married however, just because your single doesn't mean you have to be alone. It doesn't mean you have to be lonely, just means you are single. There are other relationships that can fulfill the voids in your life until Mr. Right or Mrs. Right comes along. <u>Being patient and waiting on God is not an easy thing to do. I found that my faith was constantly tested by the enemy.</u>

I remember when my daughter was about six months or so. We went to my father's house to visit. That was one of the best days of my life, to see my father in love with his grand daughter.

We went to the pool at his apartment complex. Forrest was playing in a little floating device. When we were leaving, I asked my father to get the floater. I don't swim so I needed my father to go get it. But he was so interested in Forrest, that the floater started toward the middle of the pool. I said to my father the floater, when he finally looked the floater was way in the deep end.

For the last five months I have been feeling lost, confused and sad. Not understanding what the issue with me was, my life was great! Friends, family, job and I felt I truly understood my purpose, what God really wanted of me. With all the good happening in my life I still felt sad. My emotions were like that floating device.

Every time I glanced out at the pool the floater was further away. After a point, I couldn't get it. I needed help, because I was limited. As the months went on I found myself emotionally moving further away. I no longer could snap out of it. I NEEDED HELP! God was the only one that could help me. **(2CORINTHIANS 1:9, INDEED, WE FELT THAT WE HAD RECEIVED THE SENTENCE OF DEATH. BUT THAT WAS TO MAKE US RELY NOT ON OURSELVES BUT ON GOD WHO RAISES THE DEAD.)**

I was so afraid I would slip back to the way I once was. I would get so depressed and sad that I would buy things I didn't need and some times didn't even want, to gain some sort of happiness. But this created a snow ball or domino effect for me.

Buying things was my drug of choice. Drug? Really, how? At first it worked, I would buy a pair of shoes, they come in the mail or bring them home from the store and I was happy. I smiled, put them on and walked around the house. Maybe tried on one of my dresses, which I bought in the same way. For the moment I was happy.

The problem was fixed only for that moment, I needed more. So next, it's two pairs and throw in a dress because you need clothes to wear with the shoes. Then it's a suit and I would make up a reason why I needed, not wanted it. With more and I mean more shoes. That is definitely too much, but if I could afford it I could justified this more easily. Soon I couldn't afford it and things would start to fall apart.

When that would happen, I would pull away from people and stress over being single. To the point I would believe being single was the true cause of all my woes in life. Singleness made me half of a person, even less than a person. *<u>I felt at this point drawing closer to God was what I knew to do. But feeling down not only took me away from family and friends but also God. Rekindling that love with the Lord is what was needed, then He would reveal what was next for me.</u>*

First thing I need to do is fully accept me. I did everything in my power not to be stereotyped. Stereotypical plagued woman, the stereotypes that are out there that you're only good for sex. You're only good to cook, clean or take care of other people's children. But African American women are so much more, we are much more!

We are amazing women, beautiful women, intelligent women. We are sensual, loving, humble women. We're strong and yes at times aggressive women, the ones that carry the family at least that's what I have seen in my life. I went out of my way to try to prove to others that I wasn't a stereotype.

Everything I could possibly imagine, I did. If I had it in my head, if I thought of it I did it. I was multifaceted all the time, always trying something new because I was hoping to find my niche. At times I felt like a brown mouse going through a maze. But here's the thing with that, either you go through the maze quickly and efficiently, or you go to the maze slow and you get stuck here and there. From the beginning of that maze till you come out of the other side of that maze, you're still going to be a brown mouse. Nothing is going to change. I had to learn that whether I go out there and break my neck to be the most intelligent, most successful and the most achieved woman. Or to go out there and do nothing, there will always be a circle people that will see you as the stereotype. Or the stereotypical African-American women. No matter what I did, it didn't matter. No matter what route I took, I'm still going to be an African American and I love me! If the person has already attached a stereotype to me, it isn't going to change. It isn't going to change them or I should say, the only person I can make sure that feels good about me is me. I don't have to impress anybody because God loves me the way I am. He's going to mold me to the person that I should be, the person that He intended me to be. I can't be worried or concerned about anyone else's opinion of who I should be.

<u>Ok, now I have a healthy view of myself but I'm still feeling a little alone. So now I'm thinking, does my behavior isolate me?</u>

I remember when I was a child I would isolate myself. I was always a child that withdrew and I started this behavior way back in grade school. There is always something that leads someone to isolate themselves. For me, it was being African-American in the 70s. On TV a lot of the characters were Caucasian. Nothing wrong with that however, as a young girl it was hard to see many self images as the young girls can see today. To me, the commercials seemed to be for Caucasians. I didn't notice as many black folks on TV commercials or TV shows. I think the first show that I remember on TV with black folks is Good Times. I'm not saying this is the first show, I'm just saying this is the first TV program that I watched. I'm well aware that there were programs prior to this, prior to my memory that had black folks playing in them. Good Times was the show that I really enjoyed watching also, The Jefferson's. There was also a show that I remember, a teacher show, room 77 or something like that. I'm probably wrong with the title. Also I remember the White Shadow which was a show about basketball players. Earlier than that, I remember vaguely a TV show where an African American woman played a nurse. However, these weren't shows that I normally watched. Just to show I knew of some shows prior to the ones I remember watching, some where a little before my time. But it was the one I remember first with black folks that showed a tightly knit nuclear family as well as issues some black folks could understand. Jay Jay's catch phrase was "Dyn-o-mite!" and Michael was always fighting for the black man. TV shows featuring African-Americans were far few and between, that I remember. I was in grade school in the 70's. For a lot of folks this didn't serve as a disconnect but for me it did. For me it was something that caused me to withdraw. During the early part of my life, I saw myself as ugly. At that time, my friends were Caucasian and Spanish. They had long pretty hair and they were thin. But I wasn't, I was chunky. My skin is dark I had long hair but my mother always had it in those pigtails. My hair didn't flow and at one point I had an afro, tight hair do. All in all, I wasn't the same. I saw it and I sensed it and I withdrew because of it.

I didn't have people to take the time and really talk to me, like you see nowadays. So if someone came to me today with an issue like that, regarding fitting in and feeling good in their own skin, I would ask them "What about yourself don't you like?" And, "Why don't you like that about yourself?" There would be questions I would ask, trying to get to the root of the problem. I would ask them "How does that make you feel? When people are saying things to make you feel bad? Why does that make you feel that way? Do you know that God loves you?" I didn't have anyone to say things like that to me. Folks were little bit more stern back in those days, at least that is what I remember. The attitude seemed to me was to get over it, it's going to be alright. Even Christian people I knew would give me an answer like, "You've got to have faith". A quick comment that just raced out of someone's mouth and you either caught it or you ducked. And that was it! I just think that if there was some more or I was exposed to more people that were hands-on with compassion, I think I wouldn't have gone through some of what I went through.

Now my sister was fantastic, but you know she was growing up herself. So she couldn't spend as much time as I probably needed coming up. Not that she didn't do everything. The conversations with her were wonderful she always made me feel better when the conversation was done. Always! But she was living her own life and growing up herself. She did as much as she could and I really appreciate that. I then, and still admire her.

I isolated myself by withdrawing. Don't get me wrong, I had friends. I went outside, played and stuff like that but, I also spent a lot of time with my imagination. As I got older, that time stretched into longer periods of being alone. I withdrew more from the world. I really put myself more into this fantasy type world. Where Tara was so cool, great, wonderful, fantastic and was pretty.

I ended up spending too much time in this fantasy world. Interacting with real people and having actual relationships became more and more difficult. By isolating myself, I caused myself to be single, lonely and alone. Which doesn't make things better, after a while you lose every day common ability to interact and socialize with other's.

Socializing becomes very hard work and extremely uncomfortable after a while. I find myself, even currently when I go to a lot of places. I guess some people would say "Really Tara? You go to a lot of places, are you kidding me?" But believe me, it's a lot more places than I had gone before. Just going to this or that event is a challenge. Someone on the outside looking in would say "big deal" but for me that is a big deal.

I go to church on a regular basis and I love it. Also, different meetings regarding church. I spend a lot of time there and with my family from church. This is fantastic! What people don't understand is that this is something I would not have been able to do a year or two years ago. Because I always withdrew, see my bad habits happen even when I am with the people I love the most. I just sit there and start to withdraw and I don't even realize what I'm doing. It's what I normally do, I normally did in the past. I'd sit there and look at you, acknowledging you smiling and talking but inside I'm withdrawing. The conversation starts to decrease slowly less and less until it becomes nil. Then we're just looking at each other and smiling, it's really because of me. I actually started to withdraw from the conversation, because I can really only socialize for so long and then I just automatically start to withdraw. I've been really working on that and I've gotten a lot better. In the past, many times I just wouldn't have gone, so I have gotten a lot better.

 I just have to pray to Jehovah that I get better and every day is a growing experience. By praying, God has helped me to withdrawal less and less. Socializing is just so hard for me. Funny, it kind of reminds me of that TV program, The Middle, with that little boy. He'd say something and whatever he said, the last word he said he would whisper into his chest. So for example, he would say "I had a great day" and then he'll put his head down and whisper "great day" into his chest. Then I'd say to myself "This little boy is funny." He's entertaining and I like him but he aggravates me. I think he's the cutest little thing and I love that character. I actually would watch the show mainly for his character. So why does this little boy on TV, this character aggravate me so much? Because, he's me... I saw something in him that's just a character for him but it's real for me. Now his character reads all the time. And if you tell him to do something he's so engrossed in reading, that he's not responsible with anything else but being able to read. This reminds me of myself, how I would just withdraw and pull away. I'd be so interested in doing something, whether it's listening to music or whatever, that I was completely absent minded to everything else. The only thing I didn't do was whisper into my chest, but I did talk to myself a lot at one point in my life. I don't know if it was just because I isolated myself so much that I needed to hear a voice, or what it was.

Before attending church, I would cry. Not understanding why I didn't have a husband. Thinking, those women have husbands and boyfriends. So why don't I have one? Now, so I thought, going to church would get me one. That was one of the reasons that I went to church. God is the reason I stayed. I love God! However, I'm feeling blessed for being single, because I know things need to be revealed to me. I need to work on those things because when God does provide me with a spouse, I need to be prepared. **(PROVERBS 12:4, AN EXCELLENT WIFE IS THE CROWN OF HER HUSBAND, BUT SHE WHO BRINGS SHAME IS LIKE ROTTENNESS IN HIS BONES.)**

I know this is for my betterment and I really don't want to waste an amazing blessing. I understand now, making a list of the things I need to work on. My whole brain needed to be reconstructed. When incidences happen I find myself laughing and saying to myself, not but just one year ago, I would've started a fight, started an argument, been very threatening, very aggressive and told somebody exactly where to go. One of my biggest sayings was "I'll show you exactly what spot on my butt you can kiss". That's not exactly the way I said it but that was my attitude. That was my horrible nasty attitude with everything. So when I look at the different incidences that happen I just shake it off because they don't mean anything anymore. It really didn't mean anything two, three or four years ago either but I didn't have self-control. **(2PETER 1:6-8, AND KNOWLEDGE WITH SELF-CONTROL, AND SELF-CONTROL WITH STEADFASTNESS, AND STEADFASTNESS WITH GODLINESS, AND GODLINESS WITH BROTHERLY AFFECTION, AND BROTHERLY AFFECTION WITH LOVE. FOR IF THESE QUALITIES ARE YOURS AND ARE INCREASING, THEY KEEP YOU FROM BEING INEFFECTIVE OR UNFRUITFUL IN THE KNOWLEDGE OF OUR LORD JESUS CHRIST.)**

I didn't have the ability to control myself then, but it goes to show you what God can do in your life. How He changes you for the better and what He does in your life. This is also showing me the part I played in this, that a lot of my singleness issues I brought on myself. I know at times I blamed God for things that have happened in my life. I thought to myself, "I've been looking for Mr. Right forever and God's not letting me find him". Then quickly I wake up and realize "You not finding Mr. Right Tara, is not God's fault. Look at yourself first!" What are my behaviors? What am I doing that might be repelling Mr. Right? Was I repelling Mr. Right but attracting Mr. Wrong? Mr. Right now, Mr. Right for today, maybe those are the ones you're attracting because of your behavior and repelling ways. So behavior could be something that was isolating me.

<u>Now that I have an understanding of me, just a little, it's time for me to have more appreciation for my singleness.</u>

I think to myself "It's time to take responsibility" I asked God to reveal different issues to me. Not so that I hurt or, that I'm in pain to be reminded of the things that I did, I didn't do, I could have done and I didn't or what I shouldn't have done but I did.

I ask God to reveal me to me so I could grow. So I can grow and be in a better place. Then I can look at myself, look at what I did put it behind me and move forward. It's a forward moving event here, so that's the purpose of it! There are so many times I've blamed God thinking, "I'm single I shouldn't be single this girl over here, she's a horrible person she got a man and he loves her." Or, "That's not fair these people are homeless they don't even have a roof over their heads, they got each other." That was my ignorant bitterness talking. I felt, that's not fair so why not me? Why not me… God, why don't I have anyone? Think Tara, why am I blaming God? Ok well, I am not going to blame God anymore, now I am going to blame the enemy! **(EXODUS 15:9, THE ENEMY SAID, 'I WILL PURSUE, I WILL OVERTAKE, I WILL DIVIDE THE SPOIL, MY DESIRE SHALL HAVE ITS FILL OF THEM. I WILL DRAW MY SWORD; MY HAND SHALL DESTROY THEM.')**

The enemy steps into every thing I need, everything I want, the enemy steps in and makes sure it does not happen. It's not going to happen because he will make sure it doesn't happen. Wow! What stupidity on my part. Why am I not taking responsibility for me? I'm not going to say the enemy didn't start it but I have to take responsibility for what I allowed to happen.

I remember when I was a little kid and I would have a snag on my sweater. I would go to pull it, and the older people say "No no no don't pull on it!" The thought was if you pulled that one string it could unravel the whole sweater. Well then ok, maybe it was the enemy that made that little snag but who pulled the string? ME! Now who kept pulling the string? ME! So who unraveled the sweater to whatever point the sweater was unravel to? ME! More than likely me. So what I am trying to say is, I have to take responsibility. I can't always say "I know the enemy did it." Or, "God has forsaken me" when things are really bad.

    Then I think of when my car was repossessed because I just didn't pay the car note. Now is that really God forsaken me? The enemy or me? When the mortgage has not been paid in a year and foreclosure process is starting, the argument could be "Well, I couldn't pay other bills and the mortgage too." And in that case it was the enemy and God did forsake me. No! Now, I could have had issues that the enemy had his hands in, to make things hard for me. However, God gives us the wisdom to make reasonable decisions. **(2CHRONICLES 1:12, WISDOM AND KNOWLEDGE ARE GRANTED TO YOU. I WILL ALSO GIVE YOU RICHES, POSSESSIONS, AND HONOR, SUCH AS NONE OF THE KINGS HAD WHO WERE BEFORE YOU, AND NONE AFTER YOU SHALL HAVE THE LIKE.) (PROVERBS 1:7, THE FEAR OF THE LORD IS THE BEGINNING OF KNOWLEDGE; FOOLS DESPISE WISDOM AND INSTRUCTION.)**

So did I look at my bills and see which ones need to be lowered or eliminated? What can I do without or maybe a new place to stay would be more cost efficient? God gives us the ability to make decisions. He did not forsake me, take some responsibility Tara.

Something good happened yes, God did that! God is behind that blessing. God blessed you He gave you the tools to get something done through your obedience to Him. He blessed you! Yes, you will have times where the enemy starts something, he drives a wedge between or he did this or that. But, we allowed it to keep on going. Why? Because we didn't go to God, so God could get us through it. **(2CHRONICLES 14:11, AND ASA CRIED TO THE LORD HIS GOD, "O LORD, THERE IS NONE LIKE YOU TO HELP,**

BETWEEN THE MIGHTY AND THE WEAK. HELP US, O LORD OUR GOD, FOR WE RELY ON YOU, AND IN YOUR NAME WE HAVE COME AGAINST THIS MULITUDE. O LORD, YOU ARE OUR GOD; LET NOT MAN PREVAIL AGAINST YOU.")

Again giving us the tools to complete the task, our obedience to Him is what going to give us that blessing. It's not cut and dry, the good things are God the bad things are the enemy. I am not saying that's not true. I am saying that that's not completely how it works. You don't just sit back in your life and say God's going to do all the good things and the enemy is going to do all the bad things and I take no responsibility for anything. When good things happen, I get on my knees and I pray and say thank you to God. And when things are bad I get angry with God and blame the enemy. But why God and the enemy but not myself?

Maybe I need to re-say that, because people praise God for the good, then blame Him for the bad. I interjected the enemy in this because I know the enemy exists, a lot of people don't know or don't want to believe that the enemy exists. So let me rephrase that and say that again. When things go well or things go bad people blame or praise God. What I'm trying to say is sometime or at some point you have to take responsibility for yourself. At least I had to.

And that is the reason why I'm asking God to reveal *me* to *me*. Not to feel the pain, not to be hurt, not to cry but to grow and move forward. That's what I need and in this particular situation, I'm asking God to reveal things about me.

Why? because I'm spending too much time complaining about being single and lonely. When this time could be used to celebrate being single, serving God with no distractions and appreciating the gift God has giving me. **(1THESSALONIANS 5:16-18, REJOICE ALWAYS, 17-PRAY WITHOUT CEASING, 18-GIVE THANKS IN ALL CIRCUMSTANCES; FOR THIS IS THE WILL OF GOD IN CHRIST JESUS FOR YOU.)**

However, I'm stuck on why this happened? I *need* to know why this happened. I don't believe God says, "Okay I'm going to let this child have their desire but not allow that child to have theirs." God is fair and just! **(DEUTERONOMY 32:4, THE ROCK, HIS WORK IS PERFECT, FOR ALL HIS WAYS ARE JUSTICE.**

A GOD OF FAITHFULNESS AND WITHOUT INIQUITY, JUST AND UPRIGHT IS HE.)

God gives us a gift of being single or being married. He will give this to us but perhaps we need to learn something first. For me, that's what I didn't want to accept. That's not what I wanted to hear. "Tara, you need to learn certain things to grow in certain ways first and then a gift of marriage can be gifted to you." I didn't get it before however, now I do. It makes sense to me now but it didn't before. So I no longer feel like God is holding something back from me. **(HEBREWS 6:10, FOR GOD IS NOT UNJUST SO AS TO OVERLOOK YOUR WORK AND THE LOVE THAT YOU HAVE SHOWN FOR HIS NAME IN SERVING THE SAINTS, AS YOU STILL DO.)**

I feel like God has given me so much more because I am in a position right now that I would have never been in if I had just up and got married. If I had married any of the men that I dated, I don't believe I would have been happy now. I definitely feel that I wouldn't have known my purpose, or felt I was fulfilling my purpose. So I am more than grateful. I am so grateful, it's not even funny to the level of gratefulness I feel. I truly appreciate being single at this time in my life.

<u>Although I do appreciate my singleness it doesn't stop the loneliness at times.</u>

LONELINESS

Psalms 25:16-17

*16-Turn to me and be gracious to me, for I am lonely and afflicted.
17-The troubles of my heart are enlarged; bring me out of my distresses*

2. The Aching Feeling in my soul.

Vocabulary.com defines the word loneliness as the following: 1. Sadness resulting from being forsaken or abandoned-emotions experienced when not in a state of well-being. 2. The state of being alone in solitary isolation-a state of separation between persons or groups. 3. A disposition toward being alone-being without friends or a disposition to prefer seclusion or isolation. Loneliness is the state of being alone and feeing sad about it. Your loneliness might lead you to sit at home listening to depressing songs, or it could inspire you to go out and meet people. Wikipedia defines loneliness as this: Loneliness is a complex and usually unpleasant emotional response to isolation or lack of companionship. Loneliness typically includes anxious feelings about a lack of connectedness or communality with other beings, both in the present and extending into the future. As such, loneliness can be felt even when surrounded by other people. The causes of loneliness are varied and include social, mental or emotional factors.

There are so many books out there about loneliness, singleness and accepting your singleness. How to look for the right person and what to look for. I didn't notice a lot of these books I read explains what people are going through, what they are *truly* going through. The depths of pain in their hearts.

Being single, lonely, alone and what do you do? What's the next step? My thought was just being okay with it and then I will be okay. But if I'm not okay with it then I'm selfish or something is wrong with me. Then I wouldn't really be a Christian because I couldn't accept it.

A lot of the answers I received were basically, "You are selfish Tara." Or, "You need to get over that, you need to pray or you need to read your bible more." The need to occupy my mind was a popular answer as well. In the mean time I was dying inside. Being told it will be okay with no personal connection wasn't enough for me. It wasn't that easy, I was going through something at that point. I felt a huge haze of confusion over me. I could see the truth, I could see what I need to do and, I could see what was most important. But my desire to be married was overwhelming and it felt like it was destroying me from the inside out. Don't get me wrong, I felt my spiritual life was great but my personal life, not so much.

The person I want to spend my life with I feel that wasn't going to happen and I was allowing this to destroy me. All that God has built me up to be, I felt like it's there but it's weak. Definitely feeling not happy, but spiritually *very* happy and content in many ways. Just not in my personal life and I was finding myself wanting to run back to this one ex. Feeling something was better than nothing. For what ever reason, I thought I could fulfill that husband craze. Reality is, I know he can't and Jehovah is showing me that he can't. Jehovah is showing me he is not the person, but for whatever reason I still saw him that way. I didn't get it so there was just a whole lot going on in my head about that. It was time for me to understand that yeah God freed me, He took away the pain and the tears. But unfortunately, sometimes when I got down, those feelings came back a little bit. Not back to the potency that it had in the past. The potency that it was before God freed me, but it does come back. How do I deal with it, look at it or handle it?

<u>The feeling of being without someone is hard enough, but what if mental health is involved? Is it harder? Or will there be compassion?</u>

There were two separate times I was aggressively accosted on the bus. One time with a young girl she had to be about 18 or 19 years old. Second person was a man; I wrote about that event in the last book. No need to rehash that event again.

It was just before Christmas of 2014. This young lady was out of control; you could tell there was something not right with her. She was literally hanging in swinging from the polls on the bus. She was loud and obnoxious to the point where it was just ridiculous. Before we left the bus terminal, the bus driver had to come on the bus and tell her to calm down and sit down. She some what calmed down. Then she was screaming and yelling and the whole nine all over again. Like she was out at the park somewhere or something. Then the bus started moving, at that point she calmed and sat down. I was sitting in the back of the bus, in my favorite spot. There was a gentleman that was sitting behind me but diagonal to my left. I was on the right side of the bus; she was on the left side of the bus. She was sitting in front of me diagonal to the left. There was a girl that was somewhat beside me. The girl on the bus had a friend with her. One was acting up the other one wasn't helping by encouraging it, giggling and laughing. The girl that was sitting across from me, a couple bus stops later and then this young lady entered the bus. She's sitting in the back, being quiet and then that girl that was all loud and rowdy at the beginning approaches her. Starts talking to her, I don't really know what the conversation was but I could hear her but I couldn't hear the quiet girl. The next thing you know she actually got up from the seat she was in and walked over, sat next to that quiet girl and she handed her some money. I really wasn't sure what that was about. I just kept focused on just getting home on the bus. I wasn't trying to get involved or be nosy about business that wasn't mine.

Now the same rowdy girl that began this bus journey, she starts to harass the man that was sitting diagonal behind me. Telling him she wants some money and she knows he has some money. The man started yelling and screaming for the bus driver, stating "she's harassing me she's bothering me". He was yelling for help, see at this point we're on the highway there's no place to stop. So the bus driver could've done anything anyway. He can't stop and put her off the bus. The man made such a big deal, she stopped. I think part of messing with this man for her was just purely to aggravate him. To get him going so after she got tired of him she came over to me. But she didn't approach me aggressively like she did him. Of course she didn't try to sweet talk me like she did the young lady. The way she approached me was a little more softer and a little different. When She approached me she came up to me and said "ma'am". Then she started talking a little louder just as she did when she was messing with the other people. I was praying to God saying "God please direct me, please guide and me please protect me. Because I really don't know what's going on with this girl. I don't know what's happening and please give me what I need to take care of this." **(PSALM 5:11, BUT LET ALL WHO TAKE REFUGE IN YOU REJOICE; LET THEM EVER SING FOR JOY, AND SPREAD**

YOUR PROTECTION OVER THEM, THAT THOSE WHO LOVE YOUR NAME MAY EXULT IN YOU.)

So I was praying and I think she thought I was sleeping. So she got even louder and she said "ma'am!" I shot her look that you would give to a child, the type of look my mother used to give me. Like, "if you don't sit down and be quiet and stop bothering me". It's funny because my mother could shoot you a look and that look could have had a whole conversation attached to it. She got what I was saying in that one look. She put her hands up when she saw my face, she said "Oh no, I'm not bothering with her." She went and sat back down and she didn't get up again after that but she kept talking loud, though she didn't get up and harass anybody else. When the bus stopped and she got off we all had a sigh of relief. God protected me, as well as all the people on the bus. Because I listen to what God said to do. He directed me to do exactly what He needed me to do. God knew what I did was going to deter her, calm her and down sit her down. God stopped her from the continuous harassment on the bus. What I also learned from of this situation is that you always need to have compassion for people, regardless of their actions. **(MATTHEW 9:36, WHEN HE SAW THE CROWDS, HE HAD COMPASSION FOR THEM, BECAUSE THEY WERE HARASSED AND HELPLESS, LIKE SHEEP WITHOUT A SHEPHERD.)**

I thought about that girl for a while just wondering how she was and praying that she got herself to a point where she could control herself. There was a time in my past I wouldn't give two thoughts of that girl. But today, I have a lot of compassion for her. Because of the love God has shown me I now have love for myself and can show love for others. Then I think to myself, those types of behaviors can continuously make us lonely and isolated. Those are behaviors that push others away and this is what I mean by sometimes we cause ourselves to be lonely. In her case, this could possibly be a mental health issue, causing her to act this way. Or perhaps, a chemical type issue. Whether it be synthetic drugs or a chemical imbalance, when not treated or controlled, does this cause some loneliness?

Then I think to myself, Do I cause my loneliness, through my actions, attitude or both?

I think sometimes I put myself in the position of being lonely. I put myself in a position of not only being lonely but alone. I remember one time I must've been mid to late teens. We went to a family cookout at my uncle's house, another one of my uncles had come. My uncle spoke to everyone around the table but he didn't say hello to me. So when he left the table I said to my sister "See! I do get treated differently. Because he didn't say anything to me, but he said something to everybody else at the table". My sister looked at me and said "Tara do you realize that when he came to the table you turned your head as he was saying hello to everybody. You turned your head and ignored him, so why should he speak to you? You didn't turn your head back until now that he left the table, so the person at fault was really you not him". Well of course at that age, mid-teens early mid to late teens, I didn't see that I was at fault. Now I see, it was my own fault and I put myself in a position to be ostracize.

    Another time when I was in the military, I was talking to a co-worker. He was trying to help me and he was telling me that my attitude sucked. I was explaining to him that I was a good person and I'm a good woman. I don't need to worry about changing my attitude. What he was trying to say to me was, it's the attitude that turns people off way before they even get a chance to know you. Kindly, he said to me "You probably are a good person but the attitude spoils it before they get to meet you." I could blame my arrogance on my youth but when it really comes down to it, I should have listened. The older I got the harder it was to shake the attitude and there is always those that will never let you shake it.

<u>What if I can't be happy for others, does that isolate me?</u>

What I mean is, when we have a friends, co-workers or just people in general you see on a regular basis. There were times I said to myself, "These people are horrible! They do nothing for anyone other than themselves." Or, "They are not living a good life or the right life or a life serving God. But they have a relationship, a nice one on top of it. They have a loving person that really cares about them. Something I want and I feel wow that's not fair."

I found myself to be so upset, feeling like I am still waiting, angry about this. This was just another way for me to isolate myself.

Getting upset, pulling away because I couldn't be happy for someone else. Becoming jealous of them angry and bitter. Making it worse on myself to find the person that I want to be with. **(GALATIANS 5:26, LET US NOT BECOME CONCEITED, PROVOKING ONE ANOTHER, ENVYING ONE ANOTHER.)**

Not allowing myself to be happy for someone else's blessing. Yes, <u>*someone else's blessing!*</u> I should be doing more to be happy for others. Showing the fruit of the spirit **(GALATIANS 5:22, BUT THE FRUIT OF THE SPIRIT IS LOVE, JOY, PEACE, PATIENCE, KINDNESS, GOODNESS, FAITHFULNESS, GENTLENESS, SELF-CONTROL; AGAINST SUCH THINGS THERE IS NO LAW)** so when the person God has prepared for me comes, the person that I have become is seen. Not the person that I am sliding back to due to jealousy and bitterness.

I was so quick to say someone doesn't like me or someone doesn't want to be bothered with me. But in reality, I was pulling away. I didn't want to get hurt so I pull away first. If I wanted to be a Christian that interacts with others in a Christ like manner, what can be done to make that situation better? Sometimes you have to open yourself up and it's scary it's not an easy thing to do but sometimes we have to open ourselves up. So we can get over what is causing us to pull away.

ALONE

Genesis 2:18

18-Then the Lord God said, "It is not good that the man should be alone; I will make him a helper fit for him

3. Why do I feel alone when I have God?

Alone, the Merriam-Webster dictionary describes alone as: "without anyone or anything else: not involving or including anyone or anything else: separate from other people or things. The definition continues by saying: without people that you know or that usually are with you: feeling unhappy because of being separated from other people". The online Urban dictionary defines *alone as this:* "*What you're not. Although it may seem like there is nobody there who cares about you, who is like you, or can be a friend to you, there is someone miles and miles away who would like to be there with you if they know you were calling.*"

It was Father's Day; church service was wonderful as usual. After the service everyone was fellowshipping, saying "Goodbye" and "God bless" to each other. My Pastor came up to me and said "Happy Father's Day." At first I didn't understand, why would he say that to me I'm a woman. Then he explained why he said that, because I was a single mother. I had to be both mother and father to my child, I disagreed. I felt as what my uncle said to my mother years ago, he stated that she couldn't be a father to us but she was a great mother. What he said always stuck with me, Pastor didn't agree. "Happy Father's day Pastor." I said, "God bless" and we left it at that.

I left church, one of my wonderful sister's dropped me off home. Still having the remnants of the conversation in my head with Pastor. That really bugged me, I thought to myself "Happy father's day? I'm not a man." It bothered me and then I started talking it out with God, which I often do. I said "God, you made me a woman I can't do the function in the home that a man does. That is why you made men and women different to serve different purposes in the home, right?"

The more I spoke with God, the more I could see just why Pastor wished me a happy father's day. As a single mother raising a child completely without a father, I did have to pick up the slack of what a father would be responsible to do in the family. The things Pastor is responsible to do in his own home. So yes, he would know of the things that have to get done whether both parents are there or not. Someone would need to pick up the slack, and that slack picker upper in this case is me. Now let me think, the discipline, decision making, making the decision of home repairs or doing the repairs myself. Teaching, providing, some of the more menial tasks like lawn care, car repair, and safety of my family being the most important, just to name a small few. I now see, we as single mother's are preforming the father's role in the family and single father's are preforming the mother role in their homes as well.

I think my real issue is, I am tired of being the dude! It's a hard role to play, as well as feeling robbed of being the caring nurturing mother.

I think back to when my daughter was younger, I would spend the week doing the necessities. Running here and there, with no help. It fell on me to get everything done. The weekend would come and I was just too tired to do the fun things. Not that the fun things belong to the mother's and the things not fun belong to father's. But after doing what was needed I was too tired, broke and depressed to do the things that bond a relationship between parent and child on the weekend, when I had the time.

<u>But again, responsibility time! I did as I saw, not taking the time to find the right man to have a family with if I had waited, would this be different?</u>

Being with someone prior to marriage, well now that I know what is right and wrong I think to myself what the heck did I do. Not only to myself but also to my child. Thinking a man was not necessary, in God's plan both parents are very necessary.

Having physical intimacies with someone is a big downfall and how quickly you move in the relationship becomes even more of a downfall. Here's the thing, there is no need for urgency and there's also no need for any real respect. No need for any sort of feelings for the person, no need for anything tangible or, anything emotionally tangible. I should say there's no need for you to build anything. Quickly getting together so easy and normal in today's relationships.

Like, going to a fast food restaurant. You get your food so fast there's no need nor reason for you to go, buy your food, or prepare and cook your food. Taking the time to actually wait for that meal, when you can just simply ride up to the drive thru and get one. Lickety-split, it's done in minutes and you're on your way. While this other person is preparing, cooking and waiting, the drive thru person is already eating, sitting down with his feet up and rubbing his stomach.

And I think, that's kind of a part of the problem. If we can just go and get what we want when we want it, what's the sense of actually taking time to get to know someone? Be concerned about someone, have feelings for someone, respect someone and cherish someone. There's no sense of urgency in any of those things, because I'm already going to get their quick meal.

I don't have to do anything for it and I don't have to wait. Think about it, when you wait for that meal that's prepared, someone buy's and prepares the ingredients. Cooks the ingredients, you wait for those ingredients to cook to make whatever you're making. There's the aroma and the anticipation. A satisfaction when it's done, the first spoonful or forkful. The first bite melts in your mouth, oh my goodness this is so delicious! See, you lose all that when you just go to the drive thru and get your burger and fries. You lose all that because honestly, I've eaten burgers and I've eaten fries. At no point did I sit and take a moment to just smell the aroma, of my burger or fries, nor did I care. I was too busy just inhaling it and getting rid of the wrappings. When It was gone I didn't care anymore after that and that's how I feel I was treated, as a woman. When I gave up and gave in prior to marriage.

<u>There have been times where the same ole getting nowhere has put my heart and soul in a very deep dark place. And I found staying close to good relatives and friends helped me not to check out of life. But what about those that, for whatever reason, don't have those people in their lives? Makes you think just how important a kind word or gesture really is</u>.

I remember this singer in the 80's, she was gorgeous.   She had this raspy, kind of deep but not too deep, very unique voice. Beautifully poised, elegant and wow. She commanded attention when she was on stage. I remember one-day, tragedy happened in the 90's. It was breaking news, this singer had committed suicide. It goes to show you that you could look amazing on the outside, beautifully poised, elegant, and well spoken. Just a beautiful, beautiful, beautiful human being. Talented, well thought of, the whole nine. You can appear to have it all, but inside have absolutely nothing. She was so depressed, so low just empty. She killed herself, she took her own life. And again, it just goes to show you how low you can actually get and still look amazing on the outside. So sad, she will be missed, by me and many others.

A little closer to home... Remembering a coworker that passed away. When I was much younger, just started out my career at work. I think I had just had my daughter she was brand new not even a year. Well, maybe six months but definitely not a year.

I came to work that Monday morning and her door was shut, her door was never shut. I remember another coworker coming out of her office with the saddest look on her face. We were all wondering what was going on what was happening and then it was reported to us that she had passed away. So our first thought was she must have gotten into an accident, or something along the lines. Something that was not at her own hands. When we found out that she killed herself that was hard for all of us to handle. That was really hard to handle because this was a woman that was titanium strong! She was a woman that you would've never thought had any problems.

The more we kind of poked at it, different people that knew her and those that knew her a little better. We found out that she was so depressed and so lonely, she just could not take it anymore. See, you have to understand that this was the woman you went to when you had a problem. She was so compassionate and loving and she would take you under her wing. This was a woman that would help you with anything, Anything!! A lot of people looked up to her, even people that were higher than her on the work food chain. They looked up to her. She was an amazing, amazing person! As a whole, it was very hard to understand. The fact that she was so depressed because she was lonely. And again this is the thing, on the outside, she showed the world one thing but the inside she was distraught. Not one person knew. This woman had a beautiful home, very prestigious job, she had cars, two children that loved her and all the things that come along with being successful.

She had but what she did not have was a husband. I remember someone telling me, she had started going to church. She had not in the past and she was upset even more. It depressed her to find out, the men she was attracted to or the ones attracted to her, even still in the church was only interested in sex. Which is sad because you expect so much more.

I think people don't realize that when you mislead people in this way, you not only pull them away from the world and they will withdraw within themselves. You also pull them away from God. The only one that will always be there for them! So the damage to that person is a lot graver than people think.

On a Sunday, she killed herself by going into her garage, turning on her car and sitting in it until she died. It was a really sad day for all because she was a great asset to the world! This world lost an amazing woman.

When people do not know the pain you are going through, and you assume they could not possibly understand it. Know that nothing is unique, someone understands. Then you think, how many people walking around like this, with such burdens on their hearts? Hurt and pain, so much hurt and pain that any day can be their last. Feeling that low about themselves, I've been there.

Just goes to show you, not every person who seems all together is. Issues arise, things happen, some just keep a brave face on. Doesn't mean they are ok, just means they hide it better. But when you can no longer hide it, where do you go? What do you do? **(PSALM 18:30, THIS GOD – HIS WAY IS PERFECT; THE WORD OF THE LORD PROVES TRUE; HE IS A SHIELD FOR ALL THOSE WHO TAKE REFUGE IN HIM.)**

I know how it feels to be unhappy. To the point where nothing matters anymore. A kind word, nice smile, a handshake or a warm hug, goes a long way. It did for me. Greeting others with respect, kindness and dignity.

Because we really don't know what that kindness may do for them. At the brink of letting everything go, that one act of kindness may pull him or her up from where they are. Allow God to use you in this way. **(ROMANS 8:28, AND WE KNOW THAT FOR THOSE WHO LOVE GOD ALL THINGS WORK TOGETHER FOR GOOD, FOR THOSE WHO ARE CALLED ACCORDING TO HIS PURPOSE.)**

The possibility to turn someone's whole day around and keep them on this earth for one more day.

<u>*Life, sometimes seem so tough and it is so easy to hide from the world.*</u>

<u>*But instead, being a part of something bigger than yourself is maybe the boost that is needed to make you feel better. It definitely did for me.*</u>

I participated in an event yesterday and it was just amazing. So many churches came together to serve the community. It was basically a tent fair in the effort to help the need of the community. There were different tents, one to get professional pictures taken. Many people had not had a picture taken in years, or never before with their family. Submit a resume that could be passed on to an employer that was currently hiring. Receive free groceries, free shoes, have your hair washed and cut. Provided with valuable health information and services. Enjoying a nice wonderful day, lunches were served to thousands of people and this all was free of charge. It was amazing to see God at work! There were over 2000 volunteers that took time out of their lives to happily serve other's.

(GALATIANS 5:13, FOR YOU WERE CALLED TO FREEDOM, BROTHERS. ONLY DO NOT USE YOUR FREEDOM AS AN OPPORTUNITY FOR THE FLESH, BUT THROUGH LOVE SERVE ONE ANOTHER.)

Me personally, I have been lonely, had my up's-and-down's, a little depressed. But I will say, yesterday really perked me up! This, the month of my birthday and the older I get, still being single has been making me very depressed. So when this month comes normally I'm crying, I'm upset, and I'm looking to find something to replace that sadness. Meaning, I want to go on a big vacation, buy a bunch of things or do a bunch of things. This year is the first year I wasn't as upset as the previous years. I'm still a little sad, definitely not happy about continuously growing older and not having someone to share my life with. However, no where close to how upset I was in previous years. Now, I'm okay when my birthday comes around. I believe a lot of it has to do with the fact that when events like this happen, I participate.

Going out and sharing apart of me with other's. I became one small piece of something bigger than myself. This helped me to see that I was not alone. I might be lonely, but I am not alone. Meeting new people, seeing the smiles on the children's faces, smiles on the faces of adults and getting to see people do things that I took for granted. The happiness and the pride in their hearts knowing they could overcome what ever they were going through. A day everyone involved, felt good. Truly a blessed day! So easy to lose yourself in that and your sense of being alone starts to disappear. Because you see something bigger than yourself.

I'm thankful to Jehovah for pushing me to go out on different get-togethers and participate in different events associated with my brothers and sisters at Church. Jehovah knows me and knows me well. God knows that if I'm not pushed I'm probably not going to go sometimes. Being approached in a sweet but aggressive way is the best for me. If I wasn't, it would be too easy to say no.

By going, I get the opportunity to interact with others, to get to know other people. To spark long-lasting relationships helps me not to be so alone. Instead of crying about what I don't have, I have the opportunity to celebrate what I do have.

ALONE & MARRIED

Mark 10:7-9

<u>7-'Therefore a man shall leave his father and mother and hold fast to his wife, 8-and the two shall become one flesh.' So they are no longer two but one flesh. 9-What therefore God has joined together, let not man separate</u>

4. What I have heard and what is my fear.

I happened to run across several articles, regarding feeling alone in a marriage. The point that stuck out the most to me was, *a lack of feeling close, safe, secure or connected a person may feel in a marriage. A feeling of me, not us. The feeling of not being together in the relationship but an individual in the marriage.*

I would like to start this by talking about my childhood fears, that unfortunately still linger in my adult mind. Growing up, I remember the dysfunctional relationships that surrounded me and molded my mind as to the reality of relationship. What, at some point would be my relationship. I remember one cool autumn morning, being awoken by screams. It was our neighbor in the apartments across the yard. Her voice traveled through the cold, crisp air, at least fifty to one hundred feet away. She was begging her man to stop beating her.

    Another time it was a neighbor much closer to our apartment, she screamed as well. Just before she ran out of the apartment, she asked him in between the beating "Don't you love me?" I could only imagine what her face looked like when she asked that man that question. I often thought to myself, as I went though different relationships, "does he love me?' That memory will always rip me in two.

The last one I am willing to share, was a man that had two girlfriends. One summer day, for whatever the reason those two girls beat the snot out of each other while he watched. The fight became intense and the onlookers screamed for them to stop. The guy said nothing and the girls kept fighting. Then one girl slammed the head of the other girl on the concrete. A lady in the crowd said "This makes no sense, stop it or I will call the cops!" The guy walked close to the girls and said one word, "<u>Enough</u>." The two girls stopped fighting and all three of them walked away together. It was years before I got the gist of that.

Sad to say, these events molded my mind of what I thought

a relationship was. At times these memories haunt me, to my very soul. I find myself wondering why? Why? But I know why the enemy is attacking me. To simply break my spirit and have me turn back to the world. Turn back to the empty relationships, the empty promises and the empty dreams. Well I won't! Gods promises are real! I can trust Him always, never doubting his word. I'm just sad right now but God will strengthen my spirit, my soul and my heart.

Life, being alone is tough and at times very lonely. I sit on the bus going to work fighting back tears because I no longer want to be alone. Praying for someone to share my life with. Then I think, I have so many people in my life shouldn't this be enough? Other types of relationships are wonderful and needed in my life but none are the same as a spouse. For me all other categories of relationships have room for many people. I can love many children, sisters, brothers, friends and even have affection for others as parents. But when it come to a spouse, there is only room for one in my heart not several. I can only be in love with one person. **(1CORINTHIANS 7:2, BUT BECAUSE OF THE TEMPTATION TO SEXUAL IMMORALITY, EACH MAN SHOULD HAVE HIS OWN WIFE AND EACH WOMAN HER OWN HUSBAND.)**

A friend of mine once told me she had the ability to love, or be in love with several people at once. As we debated the issue, she stated that she felt it was not harmful to be in love and in a relationship with more than one person at any given time. I however, was not falling for the "okey-doke" that hippy type of love, peace way cool man, Crap! I wasn't buying it. This thought seems to be ridiculous to me.

According to the Bible marriage is between one man and one woman, knowing this to be true, how was it possible to be in love with more than one person? What I'm to understand is, when you're in a relationship and in love with this person the goal is marriage. So, how do you marry more than one person? You don't! This debate didn't go anywhere with both sides at a standstill. However, my convictions were strengthened knowing I was walking with my God on this matter.

<u>I was thinking why couples don't make it to marriage especially after</u>

being in a relationship for long period of time?

This seemed to be my story. I would have boyfriends, especially one I can recall that just never seemed to go anywhere. After it was all said and done, I figured out why.

The best way for me to explain is this, when I was a child, I loved playing with *playdoh*. Opening them for the very first time, hearing the popping sound when the can was opened. I would take a long sniff of the p*laydoh*. I don't know why, but I loved the smell of *playdoh*. Each color was separate, green, blue, red and yellow. As time went on when I got a little older, orange, purple, and hot pink was added to the *playdoh* family. At first all the colors are separate. After a while as you use the *playdoh*, taking it out and back in the containers, there was always little pieces that would separate from the big block.

And then, I think about it, that's kind of like the problems in my relationship. It wasn't the block; the bigger problem it was the little pieces that weren't properly cleaned up. Think about it, these little pieces of different colors, there is were the problem lies. As a kid I would take the pieces and just put them together, mixing the colors. kneading the *doh* together, rolling the pieces into a big ball. Here's the problem, all of those little pieces were different problems, different issues. But after a while the individual colors weren't there anymore, just all blended together. As I continued rolling, kneading, and squished them together, I made the small pieces into a bigger ball.

So basically what I'm trying to say is, all those individual little problems or little pieces I rolled into a bigger ball, they're no longer individual problems anymore. I could no longer see the individual issue anymore. There's no distinction anymore, you have all these brightly little colored pieces that now are rolled into one big crappy brown ball. **(EPHESIANS 4:25-29, THEREFORE, HAVING PUT AWAY FALSEHOOD, LET EACH ONE OF YOU SPEAK THE TRUTH WITH HIS NEIGHBOR, FOR WE ARE MEMBERS ONE OF ANOTHER. 26-BE ANGRY AND DO NOT SIN; DO NOT LET THE SUN GO DOWN ON YOUR ANGER, 27-AND GIVE NO OPPORTUNITY TO THE DEVIL. 28-LET THE THIEF NO LONGER STEAL, BUT**

RATHER LET HIM LABOOR, DOING HONEST WORK WITH HIS OWN HANDS, SO THAT HE MAY HAVE SOMETHING TO SHARE WITH ANYONE IN NEED. 29-LET NO CORRUPTING TALK COME OUT OF YOUR MOUTHS, BUT ONLY SUCH AS IS GOOD FOR BUILDING UP, AS FITS THE OCCASION THAT IT MAY GIVE GRACE TO THOSE WHO HEAR.)
That's how my relationship ended, a doo doo brown crappy relationship. When the colors were separate in little pieces. As a kid I never took the time to pick up those little pieces and put them back into the individual containers, so they could stay fresh and be used again. In my past relationship nobody took responsibility. So the small things that could have been controlled and cleaned up became big and

caused the relationship to end. As a kid, because I didn't pick up the small pieces, I ended up with a big ball of crap that I didn't want. Nobody wants to play with the crappy brown *playdoh*.

Do I really know my role?

Now in the past I was either wearing the pants in the relationship or he was wearing the pants in the relationship. I was either completely mousy or completely aggressive. I would look back on my relationships and try to pull out of it, yeah this was a good relationship. The more I drew closer to God, and asked God to reveal things to me the revelation is, I never really had a good relationship.

Now I had bits, pieces and moments but was no good relationship. When it really comes down to it. Then I think, "Well, I had a relationship that lasted many years. It had to be a good relationship." Then I stopped and thought, "There are TV shows that run for many years but that doesn't mean it's good entertainment. This only means it ran for many years." Just because I had a relationship that lasted many years does not mean it was a good relationship. It just meant I dragged it on for many years.

It's hard because <u>now</u> I am starting to see what a relationship really is, I <u>now</u> have a working knowledge of what the responsibilities of a woman and a man are, in general. However, I seemed to have no working knowledge of what I was responsible for. I wear the dress; you wear the pants? I have my spot, my space, my responsibility. Then you got your spot, your space your responsibility? Doesn't work that way, it was just hosh posh you know pot luck, just kind of winging it to make it happen. I couldn't live that way expecting a relationship to work.

Gods' word the bible says that men are to respect, cherish and honor their wives. To treat and love their wives as they love themselves as Christ loved the church. The Bible says for women to respect, honor and obey your husbands. You are to obey your husband. **(1PETER 3:1-2, LIKEWISE, WIVES, BE SUBJECT TO YOUR OWN HUSBANDS, SO THAT EVEN IF SOME DO NOT OBEY THE WORD, THEY MAY BE WON WITHOUT A WORD BY THE CONDUCT OF THEIR WIVES, 2- WHEN THEY SEE YOUR RESPECTFUL AND PURE CONDUCT.)** Here's the wonderful part about the whole thing, if you are both doing what you are suppose to do, there is no disrespect. Wow! Can you imagine how happy people would be?

    I was one of the people running away from the very book, the very word, running from God. Amazing and complete the bible is, but I had my track shoes on running in the wrong direction. I needed to take a stand, left or right. There was a time if I was looked at wrong, by a man my attitude was, "Are you serious boo boo! No, you got to go bye!!" I wasn't giving you a chance then, I got older and I'm not looking the way I used to. So I think I have to take a little more foolishness, eat a little crow. Dealing with a lot more foolishness from foolish men. I don't want that! I don't want it! There are good Christian men out there and they are looking for good Christian woman. I am that good Christian woman!

Putting God first is a must!

Years ago when I still worked in a different office, it would have to of been about four years ago. Well, more like five or six anyways, I remember crying to a coworker about an ex-boyfriend. How he wasn't doing right about this and that. But he was a good guy and blah blah blah. Being the good Christian that she is, she said to me "Tara I know I talk to you about men and what they should have, what they should be doing. But let me just break this down to you the way I think you'll understand. Let's just talk about money, if you think about all the things he does or I should say all the things you provide for him in that house, that is yours, what's his contribution?

You know, he comes in when he feels like it. He leaves when he feels like it. Goes in your fridge when he feels like it, he eats your food. Sitting on your couch when he feels like it, he walks across your floors when he feels like it. Using your electricity to turn on your television when he feels like it. Always doing something when ever he wants to, he can lay down in your house when he feels like it. Doesn't have to be bothered with anyone if he chooses not to. Doesn't shovel, pick up leaves or mow the lawn but had no problem watching you do it. Doesn't do anything in that house when you really think about it". In my heart I knew he didn't but, her words made me snap out of it.

When I really stopped and thought about it, how much was he really doing. I was giving him too much credit for not doing anything. As she raised her voice becoming more stern with me, then she said to me "Now those things need to be paid for! Because Tara, if no one is shoveling, or doing the lawn then you must pay someone. Then think about all the other things in the house; the food needs to be bought, electricity, gas, oil for heat, has to be paid! And other things have to be paid for at some point, the wear and tear on the things that are in the house, the floors and carpet, the linoleum. What is he doing? What is his contribution in the house?" Of course I'm standing there, looking at her like she's silly. The reality is, I was the one that was silly. And then she said to me, "If you add up all the money contributions that he has given to you just this one year, divided over 365 days, what is his daily contribution?" I'm thinking to myself really quick about the monies that he had handed me throughout the year up. Until that point, it was towards the end of the year. Then I said to myself, I didn't say to her but I said to myself. We were talking about maybe the price of a cup of coffee a day, that he has put into this house. I'm not talking about you going to an upscale coffee shop, more like the cheap coffee you pick up on the fly.

Reduced down to less than two dollars a day when you think about it, and that was me being generous. And then I'm sitting there saying to myself "This is insane, what am I doing?" I think to myself, I was trying to hold on to this man because I thought he was what I wanted. I didn't want to let go!

When you come from the world and you become Christian, your views change quite a bit. You realize that if you do not have someone who puts God first, it's not going to work. I don't want to worry about what he's putting into the relationship or, what he's not putting into the relationship. This is the thing, if you don't have a man or woman that puts God first then you know what he is going to pay those bills. For me, that is not enough.

What I want is a man that is going to be _responsible!_ A man that puts God first is, going to put everything else in his life in priority. A man or a woman that does not put God first, oh yeah they're going to take care of their basic responsibilities. Take care of what needs to be taken care of at the moment, because it's what we have to do. Are they going to take all their responsibilities seriously not just partially? Not just what you feel like doing not just this or that but all of them? Not just financial responsibilities, what about the winter time? The shoveling needs to be done. Or, summer time and now the lawn needs to be done. It's after dinner and the dishes need to be done or, the floor needs to be swept. The kids need to be taking care of their homework and other things, not just financial. Errands need to be run, house needs to be clean, car needs to be maintained not just bills. Your spouse has a problem that you need to be there to help. Whether you're interested or not, even if you think it's silly or not. Even if you think your spouse is causing this discomfort for himself or herself. What about your time with your spouse, date night this is something that's important in a relationship. Just taking time to get to know each other. Quality and intimate time with each other. Not allowing the hustle and bustle and craziness of the day the week, of the month, the year to interfere with that relationship. Staying strong regarding different things that are going on in the family, taking responsibility for that. This is what I'm trying to say, this is a man or woman that puts God first! Putting God first is why all their responsibilities are in check. Taking care of each one appropriately.

Now, okay I paid the bills so now I'm going to come home. Not only am I not going to help clean, I'm not going to take care of my responsibilities at home. Because both of us are working and paying bills but I'm not going to take my responsibility at home to do my chores seriously. I've done enough outside the home. To make it worse I'm going to put my feet up and make the mess even bigger. Putting that stress and strain on one partner over the other.

I personally believe, God is who keeps marriages together. Without him, a lot of marriages that have lasted for many many years would not have lasted. Because if you're only living for yourself and you're not holding yourself responsible to anyone else, why would you do right by your spouse? How can I say this? Let me see, If I want what I want, why am I going to be obedient? Why am I going to be more compromising and show obedience to my husband, if I have no one to own up to? Example, when I wrote my first book, I said very little to anyone just wrote it. Not letting anybody see it and not saying much to anyone, there was a good shot that book could've never been publish. If I completed it or not, it would not have mattered because I didn't have to answer to anyone regarding it. Toward the end of the process I started sharing that information, letting people know. It made it so I had to own up to it. If it didn't happen, I'm going to eventually get questioned; "Oh Tara, you said you were going to write a book but you never did what happened?" It made me accountable and responsible, that's why I let people know.

I think as for married couples, when you know that your actions affect God, that puts God first, you'll think twice about it.

When I was dating I would say to myself, "You know what? I'm just going to go out there this weekend with whom I am dating and have sex". In the past that's what I did, and I had no problem doing it. Now, I think to myself, I don't want to disappoint God, number one. Number two, I don't want to disappoint me any longer. Because I know I am worth more and deserve more. God made me aware of a better life. I know that a spouse is being prepared for me. So why would I want to ruin that by just taking the easy way out? The easy way that leads to destruction. (**MATTHEW 7:13-14, ENTER BY THE NARROW GATE. FOR THE GATE IS WIDE AND THE WAY IS EASY THE LEADS TO DESTRUCTION, AND THOSE WHO ENTER BY IT ARE MANY. 14-FOR THE GATE IS NARROW**

AND THE WAY IS HARD THAT LEADS TO LIFE, AND THOSE WHO FIND IT ARE FEW.)

What I want is a quality person in my life that puts God first! I'm not downgrading anyone else. I'm just saying for me, there is a certain type of man I want in my life and putting God first is a must. Also, can I live his journey? Can he live mine? What I mean is, there's a certain way I want to live, does he feel the same? Someone that has a place on my path as well as me on his.

<u>It's been a long time coming but now I get it.</u>

Now if there's no communication, no meeting of the minds, this is going to be an issue in the relationship. I've had friends and associates say to me "What am I doing wrong? Why is this happening?" I used to find myself too embarrassed to weigh in on the conversation. I thought it would show my weakness, crying and complaining about such silliness. God has given me the strength to understand that communication is not silly, but important.

I raised my daughter as a single parent, alone. At least, it felt that way. Granted yes, I had my mother and my sisters but all in all I did the day to day work. Worrying about her needs, having or not having. Thinking to myself, "I don't want to be alone. I don't want to be by myself. I don't want to spend the rest of my life alone." So it made sense to me to start dating, put my future in my hands.

After while I had a few boyfriends behind me. No matches though, this is when I started to feel bad. What's wrong with me?

The reality is, there's nothing wrong with me per se. But I needed to find someone that has the same feelings toward God as I do. The thought of "opposites attract" didn't always work, not the end all, be all for me. No real meetings of the mind.

I would think to myself, "I'm going to keep myself closed until something more happens in this relationship. When more happens, I'm going to feel comfortable to open up." But here's the thing, if you don't open up and make yourself more transparent to the person you're interacting with, you'll never get to the point that is truly comfortable. I was a person that didn't open up, not transparent of my hopes and dreams. Thinking when I get married, I will open up to my husband, it will be easy then. I understand now that whatever reason I am holding back, isn't going to magically disappear afterwards.

I slowly realized I needed to show myself, my true self, so this potential person that may share my life knows exactly what he's getting. This is hard, very hard for me. I guarded that, meaning my heart, feelings, dreams, goals and plans more than I ever did sexually. I guess for me personally, when your initial exposure to sex is negative, you really don't care about that anymore. Didn't really matter anymore to me, so my feelings, hopes and dreams, what I wanted in life was more important to me and I kept them guarded.

I realized over the years that I've never truly given that information out to anyone, prior to writing my first book. No one knew me, the deeper part of me. I just never opened up. However, I feel like it's something that I needed to do. At some point I have to open myself to find that special person. I wasn't really willing to do it, which is not willing to give that part of me. These thoughts lead me to what society teaches all of us, only if we are willing to learn. The open, footloose and fancy free ideal of love peace and sleep with whoever you want. In the past I subscribed to this way of living but I still felt I had to hold onto something. There still needed to be something sacred for me that had to be my thoughts, feelings, hopes and dreams. So then how do I find somebody that I really want to be with that I'm really going to mesh with?

This is a long lifetime commitment, not just a five-year

event. People looking for that special person to spend the rest their life with, don't normally sit and say, "You know what, I'm going to be with this guy or girl five years and then I'll look for my next husband or wife". It doesn't work that way people are looking for forever. So they're looking for someone that is going to give them 100%! I get it now. I get it now. It's scary, but I get it now.

CONCLUSION~

I think sometimes we don't understand what a gift from God is. I really didn't understand what (gifts) were. Now I understand, you don't have to be blind to appreciate the gift of sight. Nor deaf to appreciate the gift of hearing. Have paralyzed legs to appreciate the gift of walking. Fact is, you could have the ability to hear but not really listen. God gives you that gift to truly be able to listen. This was and at times is me. Not blind but don't really have the ability to see, to really see the purpose God has given you. That's and amazing gift! To have a purpose, the most amazing gift for me. To wake and know God has a plan for me that is included in his will. What an awesome God we have! I think people, as well as I have missed out on the blessings and gifts from God being so wrapped up in this material world. **(JAMES 1:17, EVERY GOOD GIFT AND EVERY PERFECT GIFT IS FROM ABOVE, COMING DOWN FROM THE FATHER OF LIGHTS WITH WHOM THERE IS NO VARATION OR SHADOW DUE TO CHANGE.)** What I mean is, a gift was something that was wrapped in pretty packages. Or They came in the mail, or I could buy them online. Something we beg, borrow and steal to buy that's a gift... Sad! Something that you give someone from your hand to theirs. That's what I use to understand as a gift in this world.

I believe and a lot of what I have seen in this society, people don't realize the best gifts, the most important gifts, the most special gifts, are not the ones you can wrap up. No bows, no boxes, no wrapping paper and no packages necessary. These gifts are the gift of family, the gift of sharing time with someone, the gift of really being able to see beyond what you can actually physically see, your God given purpose. To be able to be touched in your heart, to be able to touch someone else in their heart. Now that's a gift! These are gifts that are overlooked, like these aren't important. What do you mean the ability to see or to touch? Why do I care about that those things? I should care because that's what is truly important. If we all practice this, if we all took the time to care more about others. Not just ourselves how much better would we all be?

Simplistic notion? Yes. But if we cared about what other people are going through, not just what we are going through, wouldn't life be a little easier? When you can give of yourself, give time and you can give of your family. Meaning sharing and bringing someone in to your family and making them feel welcome. Not just to give of your things, but to give more than that to give of your actual self. It's truly a gift to someone else. A blessing to be able to do for someone out of your heart, expecting nothing in return. That's a gift, that's not only a gift for the person that you're giving to, it's also a gift that you receive within yourself. These are the gifts that are most important, the gifts that's don't stop. God's gifts fill you, fill your heart, fill your soul and enables you to give to others.

You're never empty, you're never lacking, you're always full because you're receiving and you're giving through blessings of Jehovah God!

I say this for a reason, when you think of singleness it's hard to see it as a gift, when your desire is not to be single. But when you think of everything I just said regarding giving of yourself, those are wonderful blessings and gifts that you share with others. Not only fulfill something within them but, fulfills something within yourself as well. This is when you understand how being single is a blessing.

Now I see my life in a positive way, I can recognize being single as a blessing! Originally I didn't see the blessing. As I interact with people and shared with them, not only sharing of my time also my life. My brothers and sisters at church, sharing their lives with me. Time spent with their families, their personal space. Being invited to a meal, maybe a movie, to the park. Everyone intermingling together having fellowship. **(PHILEMON 1:6, AND I PRAY THAT THE SHARING OF YOUR FAITH MAY BECOME EFFECTIVE FOR THE FULL KNOWLEDGE OF EVERY GOOD THING THAT IS IN US FOR THE SAKE OF CHRIST. ~ 1 THESSALONIANS 5:11, THEREFORE ENCOURAGE ONE ANOTHER AND BUILD ONE ANOTHER UP, JUST AS YOU ARE DOING.)** Enjoying each others company has shown me how blessed I am to be single. To be able to volunteer for things that perhaps I couldn't have done if I were married. To go places and do for others at the spur of the moment, perhaps I would not be able to do if I were married.

I'm not saying that being single is what I want forever. What I am saying is that God gives you gifts at the time of your life when you truly need them. Even when you're not aware of what you need **(MATTHEW 6:8, DO NOT BE LIKE THEM, FOR YOUR FATHER KNOWS WHAT YOU NEED BEFORE YOU ASK HIM.)** and even when you truly feel you don't want that particular gift at that time. God however, knows what you need at every point. Every time and place of your life. It takes a while and it took me a while to understand however, singleness for me is truly a blessing. There is a perfect time and season. Only God knows what that perfect time and season is for you!

SCRIPTURES USED:

2CORINTHIANS 12:9
PSALMS 37:4
PSALMS 37:5
PSALMS 37:7

SINGLENESS~
1CORINTHIANS 7:8-9
2CORINTHIANS 1:9
PROVERBS 12:4
2PETER 1:6-8
EXODUS 15:9
2CHRONICLES 1:12
PROVERBS 1:7
2CHRONICLES 14:11
1THESSALONIONS 5:16-18
DEUTERONOMY 32:4
HEBREWS 6:10

LONELINESS~
PSALMS 25:16-17
PSALMS 5:11

MATTHEW 9:36
GALATIANS 5:26
GALATIANS 5:22

ALONE~
GENESIS 2:18
PSALMS 18:30
ROMANS 8:28
GALATIANS 5:13

ALONE & MARRIED~
MARK 10:6
1CORINTHIANS 7:2
EPHESIANS 4:25-29
1PETER 3:1-2
MATTHEW 7:13-14

CONCLUSION~
JAMES 1:17
PHILEMON 1:6
1THESSALONIANS 5:11
MATTHEW 6:8

BIBLE USED:
ENGLISH STANDARD VERSION

DICTIONARIES USED:
THE MERRIAM WEBSITE DICTIONARY.
THE FREE DICTIONARY (ONLINE).
VOCABULARY.COM
WIKIPEDIA.
THE MERRIAM-WEBSTER DICTIONARY.
THE ONLINE URBAN DICTIONARY.